Awakening the Laughing Buddha within

By Joe Hoare and the Barefoot Doctor

Text copyright © 2013 Joe Hoare and the Barefoot Doctor

www.joehoare.co.uk

www.barefootdoctorglobal.com

ISBN 978-1-300-97947-0

Thank you

I have so many people to thank. I am reminded of the Carl Sagan quote: "If you wish to make an apple pie from scratch, you must first invent the universe". I am aware of so many influences that have shaped this book.

First of course is my family for their boundless support. At times I felt I was wandering in the desert and their support during this phase – the gestation – was invaluable.

Secondly, all my friends and colleagues in the healing world and Mind Body Spirit scene whose insights have shaped my life beyond recognition. To me, it is now one of life's givens that we are spiritual beings having a human experience. How I used to scoff at that kind of statement.

Thirdly, all my friends and colleagues in the laughing community are a source of continued inspiration. Our time is coming. The idea of laughing for health, happiness and wellbeing has unassailably taken root.

Fourthly, there is a special band of pioneers who know who they are. The pioneering role is sometimes a lonely one and it has been good to share kindred spirit moments with you.

Fifthly, my 'boys'. I am lucky enough to live in the same city as two of my oldest friends. You can't beat an old friend.

Sixthly, there was a decade with June Burrough and the Pierian Centre which became a byword for warm, supportive, insightful excellence.

Finally, though they don't realize it, all my squash partners. To laugh, be good-natured and zen as the adrenaline pumps your system and you race around a tiny box is the most demanding and rewarding practice I've found.

And thank you everyone else, because you've all contributed too. *Joe.*

Introduction.

I've produced this book with my insightful friend the Barefoot Doctor to encourage, inspire and give you heart on the zigzag journey through life.

For my part, it is a synthesis of 20 years of self-development, and a previous 25 years of conscious adult awareness. Based on the premise that laughter precedes and boosts happiness, it is a guide, a story, a journey and a manual so you can awaken your own Laughing Buddha within. Its simple steps have transformative effects. They will empower you, assist all other heart-opening and loving-kindness practices, and establish you firmly as the captain of your own life.

Here in the West an enormous cultural, psychological and spiritual transformation is occurring. Increasing value is being put on the quality of our inner experience as well as outer achievement. Through disciplines like Positive Psychology we are beginning to recognize the importance of intrinsic values as well as extrinsic ones. We are beginning to realize how important it is to enjoy the journey.

We are beginning to understand how the Quantum world is the scientific equivalent of the ancient Hindu model of 'Indra's net' and that we are all connected. We are coming to realize that the quality of our inner life is important for the world and not just for ourselves, and that in fact there is no separation at all. 'I am in you and you are in me', says Deepak Chopra, meaning we are all inextricably inter-connected on an energetic level. The quality of our thoughts and emotions, and the intentions behind our actions, color not just our life but in this inter-connected way we're now beginning to understand, all life. This is not narcissism, nor indulgent introspection, but both modern physics and ancient knowledge. It means every one of us is a contributor to the happiness, sanity and quality of life in the world.

We all matter.

To those who don't know me I often appear to be a Pollyanna figure, cheerful, optimistic, and fairly easy-going, almost in denial. The truth is that the reason I am now an incorrigible optimist is because I've bled, suffered, been crushed and broken-hearted, manifested and faced down my greatest fears, and have emerged joyful.

Not one of my past experiences has maimed me or in any way diminished me. On the contrary, I look at them all and say 'thank you'. All the scars on my heart and consciousness have been mended in the Japanese tradition of kintsugi, 'Golden Seams'. In that tradition broken porcelain is repaired with gold and so can become even more wonderful than before. My own scars are not places of weakness but of strength, they are golden seams. They are expressions of a life lived, loved and healed, and these are the qualities I look to bring to life in others. After a typically tortuous journey I have come to a place where I'm happy to use my own story to give people hope, courage, strength, compassion and most of all to encourage open-hearted, joyful connection, both with themselves and others.

To those wondering how to do this, how to awaken your Laughing Buddha within, I say the most important qualities are gentleness, kindness and patience. The more you develop these qualities, the richer your own life experience becomes. You experience more love and delight, and you experience them more regularly and frequently. Yes, you also have to be smart, tough, strong, irrepressible, articulate and so on but these are secondary. I have encountered so many people who were using these as their primary tools in what appeared a successful life when suddenly they had a crisis and had to embark on their inner journey. They then found they needed all the kindness and compassion qualities to heal. The qualities of toughness, strength, smartness and indomitability were all useful but they were servants to kindness, compassion and self-love.

This is also my own experience, from my attempted suicides, my insomnia hell, and my perfect Fear moment, which I write about later. What matters most is to bounce back, to keep saying 'yes', to be prepared to experience hurt again and again. It is vital not to let past pain in any way diminish your present and let fear overpower dare. You have to dare to keep turning up in your life, learning and getting wiser, and to keep letting go of your ego and your 'story' one melt at a time.

This book will help you.

Developed in collaboration with that master of modern Taoism, the Barefoot Doctor, it draws together insights from two robust bodies of knowledge and creates a superb framework to enable you to combine your Laughing Buddha and Taoist practices. It's a powerful combination, injecting F1 hybrid vigor into the page and reinforcing the waking up process.

Don't be deceived by the apparent simplicity of the exercises. In psyching yourself up to keep persevering it helps to take baby steps. This is not 'baby' in the sense of 'not grown up' but in the sense of one small step after another. There is good research and history to encourage setting small, achievable targets that you actually meet because this encourages you to keep persevering. Just keep moving forwards. This is essential to help you through the dark lean phase between your initial enthusiasm and your place of confirmed knowing. You are likely to have an early affirming experience which shows you beyond any doubt the value of practice.

Next you'll be in that indeterminate phase after your initial flush, where you need what the Dalai Lama terms 'effort' to keep going. It can feel like hard work because it's taking time and effort and you can't see any more results. There might even be disappointments. Hang in there. This is your crucial foundation phase. Soon you will have another experience which shows you beyond any doubt that your practices are helping. You just have to keep going through that middle phase. The good news is that it's not really very long. If you keep your daily practice going for maybe only 20 days, you'll have set up your new good habits. Just keep going. Your Laughing Buddha within is waiting for you.

As you wake up your Laughing Buddha within, you influence your energetic environment for the better at any moment you choose, and the more you do so, the more you see and experience this. You might astound yourself at the effect your practice has especially when you do it invisibly and inaudibly. An invisible smile given as a random act of kindness can elicit a visible one even from strangers. As you practice this you'll experience this yourself.

What follows in this book is a journey with exercises, science, ancient insights, and unexpected, spontaneous feedback. Enjoy!

And now it's over to the Barefoot Doctor.

Barefoot Doctor's introduction

Whenever someone close to me has died, I've experienced receiving an inheritance of sorts, by way of a direct cross-dimensional telepathic download of that person's particular gift for me. When my teacher of 'consciousness' and psychotherapy, RD Laing died, I inherited the ability to think deeply and in a relatively straight line, and to write - I also inherited the pen he wrote his books with. When Frank Kramer, my teacher of unconventional wisdom, died, I inherited the facility to disseminate unconventional wisdom, along with the stratagem for creating a viable platform from which to disseminate it - and I also got back the hair clippers I'd lent him. When my beloved PA, 'Naked Nurse', Carrie Carter died just recently, I inherited a healthy dose of her magnificent compassion. And when my dad, Victor, died, I inherited the capacity to laugh at every eventuality - I also inherited his laugh: the sound of my laugh became the sound of his laugh - I actually inherited my father's laugh. This was useful from the start as, unlike most people who inherit money on the death of a parent, I inherited a debt, and the laughter helped me take it lightly, as it's helped me take lightly all the various trials and tribulations ever since.

It's not as if I hadn't laughed at the twists and turns of life's theatre hitherto, but now it's a full-blown, raging default mode.

Daniel, my teacher of Chinese medicine, to whom I was apprenticed for nearly four years many decades ago, wouldn't even let his students take the qualifying exam till he'd heard them making patients laugh on a regular basis. He taught that laughter is the most potent medicine of all - before acupuncture, acupressure, herbs, bone-setting, massage, therapy and all the rest of it, laughter must happen for the patient to begin the path of recovery.

Patria, my 'fairy godmother' (everyone should have one), during a conversation about the woes of the world one day, also many decades ago, in which I was earnestly expressing my concern for the huge levels of bovine-like stupidity I was witnessing in the world, asked whether I imagined God found it all amusing. I shook my head. In return she shook her finger admonishingly, "If you think God's got no sense of humor, think again, young man" - and made me laugh.

Pragmatically speaking, laughter heals you by causing your diaphragm, the large transverse muscle at the upper abdominal level that provides your lungs their bellow motion, to flicker repeatedly - to contract and release rhythmically - until all the tension you've been holding in your solar plexus dissolves. This tension otherwise accumulates there because this is the region of the body responsible for processing incoming information, whether in the form of food, which is then transformed into nutrients in the bloodstream, or in the form of ideas, which are then transformed into nutrients for the mind.

The first thing that happens when any new packet of information enters your system is resistance. This is natural and as it should be. If we weren't with an innate propensity to resist the new we'd not be here in form to discuss it in the first place: we'd have just continued to be undifferentiated parts of the continuum of swirling atoms and subatomic particles comprising our universe. So when new information arrives, whether as food or ideas, the first thing we do is resist. And this resistance builds up a residual tension in the soft tissue of the solar plexus region. This tension stimulates the release of cortisol, the stress chemical, which is highly addictive, and so leads us unconsciously to compound the solar plexus tension, thus leading to a vicious cycle.

This can be effectively addressed over time by becoming mindful of the build-up and using mental focus to relax the area progressively more, but there's nothing like a bout of belly-laughter for a quick release and if practiced regularly will have profoundly beneficial effects. This is also true for crying, or course, which is equally effective for dissolving the tension, as it causes the diaphragm to flick in the same way as laughter does.

All three devices subsequently give rise to an endorphin release - the endogenously produced happiness chemical - and so give rise to a virtuous cycle. And while developing mindfulness and mental focus to reduce tension is advisable as a long-term happiness strategy, of the other two, laughing is obviously preferable to crying, if you have a choice, because crying makes your eyes look scrappy and laughing is fun.

And you do have a choice. You can actually train yourself to laugh and remain in the laughing state (whether internally or externally) perpetually, constantly seeing the joke, always at one with the Laughing Buddha, the God or Tao informing and animating this entire spectacle we call life.

Which is why I was so happy when Joe invited me to collaborate on this wonderful book. As well as being one of the world's great gentlemen and a most affable and noble fellow, Joe is the consummate laughing yogi. I've watched him work a room and transform an atmosphere from one of mild fearfulness to one of powerful bonding in collective joy in a matter of minutes, simply by getting people to divest themselves of their adult veneers of stiffness and pretense and become as little children, laughing, hugging and all but skipping for joy.

And my part - the reason Joe called me in - is to bring you the practical 'exercise' aspect culled from the magnificent ancient Taoist system of wellbeing I practice and teach, a central theme and tenet of which is the encouragement of a perpetual state of laughter or at least laughter-readiness. He felt - and I agree - that these exercises will help you more easily embody the Laughing Buddha within. They comprise visualization skills, breathing, manual release technique, realistic positive thinking technique, and the method of repositioning consciousness within the body, to augment the capacity for spontaneous laughter at the drop of a hat.

These exercise sequences are presented in progressive training form, so that at the end of each chapter you'll find yourself reviewing the previous exercise sequences and integrating them into the next one, all building cumulatively to a crescendo of eternal laughter.

You'll have noticed in the preceding, incidentally, a tendency to mix my religious and spiritual nomenclature, using variously and interchangeably the terms *God, Tao, Buddha* and so on. I suggest there is nothing contradictory about this and that all are merely terms expressing the ineffable, none ultimately sacrosanct in themselves. In any case I am, and strongly advocate being, a spiritual slut.

You may wonder what metaphysics of any kind has to do with learning to have a good laugh, but I suggest once this all becomes second nature to you, when in the midst of a proper belly laugh, you ask what could possibly facilitate such an unlikely event as being on a life-supporting planet in human form laughing your head off, if not something slightly beyond the obviously physical (the literal meaning of metaphysical).

You might have also discerned a subtle tendency not

to take myself too seriously. And I offer this as a pre-exercise before we even begin the book: stop taking yourself so seriously immediately.

See you shortly in the main body of the book.

Chapter 1. How it all starts

'Because of your smile, you make life more beautiful.' Thich Nhat Hanh

No one, fortunately, has ever described me as a Laughing Buddha.

However when my friend Will described me as a laughing yogi, I did listen although my resistance hackles immediately started to bristle. I have a deep and innate suspicion of terms like 'satsang', 'guru' and similar titles in the contemporary mind, body, spirit scene and instinctively shy away from them. When I got home I looked up both the Wikipedia (of course) and Oxford English Dictionary definitions of 'yogi' and I found its simplest definition is 'a practitioner of yoga'. Further re-reading of basic terms reminded me that the fundamental definition of yoga is 'union'. The aim of the different yogic practices, traditions and disciplines is to help yogis achieve increasing degrees of union: of body with breath, and mind with body for example, up to a level of union with the universe and the consequent sense of peacefulness and harmony.

Using these definitions, the term laughing yogi translates into someone who uses laughing for health and wellbeing, and to achieve a sense of harmony with the universe.

I mentally commended Will for his perception and accuracy because after a typically zigzagging journey, that is exactly what I now do, both for myself and for others. After almost twenty years exploring personal development and therapeutic techniques which have included Chi Kung, NFSH Healing, Breathwork, 5 Rhythms, Overtone Chanting, Reiki healing, Meditation & Visualization, Archetype healing, Massage, Dowsing, Contact Improvisation, Tai Chi, Free your Natural Voice, and others, I found the practice of laughing works best.

The Laughing Buddha is an archetype of happiness, abundance, and wisdom of contentment. It represents generosity and openheartedness, qualities we all possess and have the potential to develop. Everything that follows is to help you develop your own laughing yogi practices and awaken your Laughing Buddha within.

On a conscious level my own journey started with my first grown-up thought. I was 15 and had just been expelled from Eton for repeatedly getting caught drinking, getting drunk, breaking out of the house at night, and the final straw - being in possession of an air pistol that actually belonged to someone else, the younger brother of a now-well-known environmentalist. My father was taking me to see a Vocational Guidance Counsellor and on the way over, Dad asked me if I had any idea what kind of career I wanted. I opened my mouth and the words that popped out were 'I want to help people'. He asked me if I meant being a psychiatrist and I replied no, it wasn't quite like that but I knew in my gut that I had no interest in a career like law, investment banking or politics.

I don't remember any more about that conversation but the 'I want to help people' bit stuck in my mind for a long time, gestating. It finally burst out of my consciousness, like the alien from John Hurt's chest, about 25 years later in the first healing circle I attended. It was on the first day and we were starting to learn about distant healing. With his permission, we were about to send some distant healing to an emotionally un-expressive husband who had never been able to tell his wife he loved her, even though he could tell his children he loved their mother. That story resonated profoundly with me as in hindsight I was a perfect model of emotional repression and immaturity. Hearing his wife tell the story, I felt it was me and my story. As soon as the healing started, the turmoil that had started to well up in me and that I'd been desperately trying to hold down ripped its way through my defenses. My heart was ripped open and I burst into uncontrollable tears. I sobbed and sobbed, overwhelmed and yet also relieved. My shell had shattered, and that cathartic breakthrough redefined my priorities in one heart-opening nano-second. Through that crisis I had 'woken up' in the way Gurdjieff, the Russian mystic, described. I had pierced the veil and had a direct personal experience of the spiritual world behind the material and physical one. My life, my real life, had started.

I have learnt my most valuable lessons from the crises and catastrophes in my life because like the snake shedding its skin, they generated life-changing opportunities. Painful though they were from the usual heart-ache and heart-break, to three suicide attempts, insomnia hell, being bullied, complete material loss, shame and fear, I have allowed myself to learn from them all. I have been knocked to the ground many times and my previous ways of thinking have been comprehensively shredded. It is now my experience that life is unimaginably different from what I grew up to believe, and because I manifested my greatest fears and emerged from them both tougher and kinder, I feel lucky. I now know that words like impossible, unthinkable and unimaginable are arbitrary and relative, and that when we give ourselves permission, miracles happen. I have experienced three sublime times in my life when for a few months, everything was perfect. The first time in my late teens was a surprise, the second time about 20 years later had an element of recognition, and the third time, in my forties, I savored because I knew it would pass. I look forward to the next one.

I now do everything I can to encourage others to grow too without necessarily having to experience the extremes I did. You don't have to create an enormous crisis before you start extracting the lessons and replacing your rigidity with flexibility. Because this experience has been seared into my consciousness, I feel increasingly relaxed about encouraging others to flex rather than break, and over the years my research has shown how many cultures in the past have had the same insights.

After this initial catharsis, I put all the time and energy I could spare into exploring this new world. I was curious, insatiable and soaked up as much information and as many experiences as I could. Having started my life in the Christian tradition, I became a spiritual magpie. I delved into many traditions and explored many practices, and now my overall view of spiritual practice is summed up by the 7th principle of Huna: 'Effectiveness is the Measure of Truth'. In other words, 'does it work'? I have found these awakening your Laughing Buddha practices work better than any other, as have other people too.

At the heart of awakening your own Laughing Buddha within is genuine, good-natured laughter. When we laugh in a genuinely good-natured way, we are capable of experiencing harmony, i.e. union, with our self, with others and with all life around us. With practice we can access this very quickly. We can all become skilled at bringing all our attention into the present moment in a joyful way. This gives us the potential to become an oasis of harmony in the discordant strife we sometimes find ourselves surrounded by. Sometimes that strife is with other aspects of our self, as we probably all experience regular conflicts between heart and mind. We get torn between what we think we ought to do and what feels right. Sometimes that strife is with our family and other relationships, and sometimes it is with a grim set of physical circumstances. Being able to access an inner pool of peacefulness and harmony no matter what is happening around us is a wonderful skill to develop. As you awaken your Laughing Buddha within, this gets easier.

A precursor of what's to come, if you can manage it, is to take a big breath, hold it, and let it out with a good-natured chuckle. Not to worry if you can't, there's a gentle progression as you go through the book.

We are increasingly familiar with the benefits that laughing brings. One of the most telling examples is Patch Adams, the US doctor portrayed by Robin Williams in the film of the same name, who has been using laughter as a treatment with his patients at the Gesundheit Institute since 1971. This is both a pioneering and enduring organization and it is worth exploring some of their values because there are signposts and clues for all of us.

- Patients are treated as friends.
- The health of the staff is as important as the health of the patients.
- Care is infused with fun and play.

One connecting thread with these values is emotional warmth and another is lightness. Both of these are core practices for waking up your own Laughing Buddha.

We are often impelled to learn new practices and develop new skills when we experience crises. The good news is we ourselves don't need to experience the full depths of such crises before starting to learn these inner harmony techniques. We can learn from observation, by extension and by other people's experiences. This means these techniques are easily accessible to everyone. You too can awaken your laughing Buddha within by following simple steps.

The starting point and simplest exercise, as Thich Nhat Hanh's quote at the start of this chapter suggests, is *SAW* – smiling at will. It is a key skill that can be used at any time and in any circumstances. It can be used to keep your optimism levels high, as well as a general top-up for your mood and outlook. It is one of the easiest personal development steps you can take, requiring minimal effort. It is baby step one.

There are two aspects to this smile, and the thread that connects these aspects is making it genuine and good-natured.

Can you just do it, now, as you're reading this? Stop for a second, relax your face, and smile a gentle smile. Hold it for at least 5 seconds before reading on.

To make it a bigger exercise, it helps to do some facial warm-ups. Facial massage and stretches especially of the jaw muscles but also including forehead, eyes and cheeks, wake up and loosen the grip of your facial mask. Anyone who is a singer will recognize these warm-ups as they bring your whole face to life and get it flexible and expressive.

The next step is to smile in a genuine and good-natured way. The size of the smile is unimportant as it can be very small and still be effective. When it is genuine it involves two sets of facial muscles, zygomaticus major and in particular orbicularis oculi. These sets of muscles are around our mouth and eyes and when we smile a genuine smile, they automatically soften and express and communicate warmth, the 'milk of human kindness.' This is the Duchenne smile. You can tell its genuineness by how it feels.

The final step is to keep this genuine smile on your face for 15 seconds. This takes practice because typically a smile is gone within a couple of seconds. Some people find it helpful to use the power of their mind by remembering or visualizing happy experiences, or by remembering and hearing the sound of laughter with their inner ear. Others are experiential and are happy just to do the practice.

Can you do it again now?

One of the revealing studies on the power of the smile was done in 1988 by the psychologist Fritz Strack and his colleagues, and involved rating how funny people found *Far Side* cartoons. Before rating them, one group was asked to hold a pencil in their teeth, no lips, and the other was asked to hold the pencil in their lips, no teeth. With their pencils held in their respective positions, the group with the pencils in their teeth, no lips position found the cartoons much funnier than the lips, no teeth group. Effectively the teeth, no lips group had their faces in the position of a smile, and the lips, no teeth group had theirs in the position of a frown. The study showed that simply having their face in the position of a smile affected not only how funny people found the cartoons, but also that these feelings of enjoyment endured after the experiment had ended.

This practice works on a biochemical and psychological level. Biochemically, when we smile we trigger the endorphin effect and revitalize our whole body.

Psychologically when we engage mindfully and deliberately in a life-enhancing activity, we experience a sense of control of our life, and possibly a sense of liberation. That is why your first Laughing Buddha wake-up step is this simple twice-a-day, morning and evening smiling practice. Put a smile on your face and maintain it in a genuine and good-natured way for 15 seconds. If it helps, use the power of your mind to recall happy memories or anticipate future delights.

You can of course smile lots more, and I hope you do. It is beautifying inside and out.

This comment arrived unexpectedly in my inbox one day.

'I just wanted to let you know how I have been getting on since I came to the last Laughter Club meeting.....I have been following your instructions to smile first thing every morning and last thing at night. Wonderful!

I have to say that I have felt a real change in me. My face seems lighter and I feel more positive.

Last week whilst reading the news on Bristol hospital radio my fellow news-reader read a funny story and I laughed until I cried and neither of us could finish the news through constant giggling. I do not remember the last time that I laughed that much and I wanted to thank you for giving me the courage to laugh out loud again.'

Now we've defined the quality of the smile, here is Barefoot Doctor's Exercise Sequence 1

As well as referencing happy memories to help elicit a smile, relax your body, slow down your breathing tempo and picture this: a smile seemingly with an *a priori* existence all of its own, a very tiny and discreet smile, nestling right down between your legs bang in the middle of your pelvic floor, equidistant between anus and genitals. As you focus on it, breathing slowly all the while, watch it grow progressively larger with each passing exhalation. See the smile grow larger and larger until it fills your entire pelvic bowl, all the way up to waist level. And larger and larger still, until it fills you all the way up to your chest. And larger and larger still, until it fills your entire being, all the way beyond the tops of your ears, so that your whole body is now one giant smile.

Stay with that, enjoying the subtle endorphin release for a few breaths, then ever so lightly, start to appreciate the huge Laughing Buddha to whom the smile belongs. You have now become the smile on the Laughing Buddha's face, which, you must admit, is quite an achievement for a mere mortal.
Return to this contemplation briefly yet frequently through the day, as you work, rest and play - and through the night too. Fall asleep doing it and you'll dream the jolly dreams of the Laughing Buddha the whole night long and awake

enlivened and restored from the ravages of the world in the morning light.

Chapter 2. What's so funny?

'We don't laugh because we're happy, we're happy because we laugh'. William James

Usually when we think about why we laugh, it is because we find something funny. We laugh at jokes, at banana skin incidents, because something tickles our funny bone and because of our own particular sense of humor. In these situations our natural laughing reflex takes over and we simply laugh. Because of the quirkiness of our sense of humor, this can and does happen at inconvenient moments. For example, at school on one occasion the whole class was set to read 'My family and other animals' by Gerald Durrell. We were all sitting there reading, in silence, and I started to find the book really funny. Finally I just couldn't help it and I laughed out loud. The master fixed me with a mock stern look before saying 'I was waiting for someone to do that!' I felt relieved because I expected to be in trouble, slightly pleased with myself for having been the first person to laugh out loud, and very happy not to have to bottle it up any longer. I laughed because I found the book funny, and the more I laughed, the funnier I found it.

Culturally, this is how we do it in the West. We laugh because something is funny. Because so much of our culture is framed by the crucifixion, it is set against a backdrop of great seriousness. You can laugh for all kinds of good reasons, but you return to a baseline of serious. When we laugh because something is funny – and that of course varies for each of us – it can be a distraction, can cheer us up, can entertain and amuse us, speed up our return to health and give us good heart, all the wonderful things that happen when we laugh. The crucial aspect here is that to be able to access all these benefits, first of all we have to find something funny. Our laughing is dependent on humor.

But what if we can find a way to laugh first, before finding something funny?

We have probably all had the experience of laughing and then finding you're laughing more and more. Someone I know told me of a long-standing friend who comes to stay with him. They have known each other a long time and they hugely enjoy each other's company and laugh lots. What they both find is the longer they're together, the more they laugh. Even tiny, inconsequential events can trigger almost uncontrollable hilarity, and they reach the point when even one tiny look can start it all over again. Laughing more makes them laugh more.

As you wake up your own Laughing Buddha within you can use lots of genuine, good-natured laughter to help you enjoy your journey more. In the previous chapter we saw how smiling at will starts to liberate your consciousness, and that simply doing the 15 second morning and evening smiling exercises can make it easier to laugh more. The smiling makes life situations funnier, and the key becomes accessing your own genuine, good-natured smile quickly and easily many times a day. Practicing your soft-faced, genuine 15 second smile is vital and hopefully enjoyable.

Laughing Buddha laughter is also a way to experience and develop peacefulness, health and happiness. One of Dr. Madan Kataria's insights, his inspired genius moment that impelled him to set up Laughter Clubs and then Laughter Yoga, was that the benefits of laughing come from the act of laughing, not from a sense of humor. As a GP he realized more often than not he could do more for people by prescribing daily doses of laughter rather than medication, and so in 1995 Laughter Clubs were born.

In 1996 Private Eye published an article in their 'Funny Old World' section which caught my eye, and which I still have. It also caught other people's eyes too including John Cleese who featured the laughing clubs of India in his 2001 series 'Human Face'; to date there are over 10000 clubs world-wide.

The American psychologist William James noticed in his work in the late 19th century that laughter precedes and boosts happiness. The key becomes to start with the laugh, not the funny. Although you can start with the funny to start the laugh, crucially, you can also start with the laugh to trigger the funny. You can laugh first. The Kahuna, the Hawaiian shamans, also realized this many centuries ago and developed exercises where you play with your laughter sounds as a morning practice.

I started using laughter as a practice inadvertently. One of my psyche-melting breakthroughs occurred when I 'discovered my natural voice' with Chris James, the Australian 'Free your natural voice' maestro, and so broke free from the restrictive vocal prison I'd been living in for the previous 30 years. After experiencing my initial vocal liberation, I knew I had to keep practicing to extend my own vocal freedom. I also wanted to be able to teach others, so I needed to practice. I was spending a lot of time driving so I did my breathing, sighing and groaning exercises whenever I drove. I learnt overtone chanting, throat-singing, and toning which is holding and sustaining single vowel sounds. Besides finding them ecstatic, liberating, meditative, connecting, consciousness-expanding and heart-opening, I also found them a good stress-buster.

One of my own personal demons used to be insomnia and a trick I picked up while exploring toning was that if I woke in the night and started fretting, toning helped calm my mind. This was easy to do when I was living alone and of course is easier to do when you don't have a partner in your bed who is happily in the land of nod. For preference you don't want your personal development practices to become a domestic battleground.

What I discovered with the middle-of-the-night night toning was it didn't need to last long to work and no more than 5 to 10 minutes was usually plenty. It was long enough to alter my state of mind and sleep always came shortly. Looking back now, three clear reasons it worked are because it was psychologically proactive, it was oxygenating, and it caused my breathing to deepen and therefore relax.

I developed other Laughing Buddha practices when my life was going through a particularly unfunny phase. My greatest fear in life, the perfect fear moment I referred to earlier, had been the prospect of financial insecurity and losing my savings. Because I focused on that so much and for so long, naturally I made it come true. The adage is 'what we focus on, expands' and I focused on a pit and fell into it. Because I tend to do things fully, I made sure it happened at the same time as I lost my wife, family, home and career, and I felt more scared and ashamed life than I ever had before. Naturally this impinged on my sleep and I sometimes woke in the small hours with night-time terrors. I had moments when I felt beside myself with worry and fear, and in those moments I used to laugh, not because it was even slightly funny but because I needed to do something proactive. It was surprising, as with the midnight toning, how little laughing it took to regain a sense of balance and equanimity. Any laughing sound would do and it didn't matter if initially it was fake because provided I kept my willingness going, it soon turned into the genuine thing. 'Fake it till you make it' worked under extreme pressure.

The first time this worked I wondered if it was coincidence but when it worked every time, I knew I had stumbled across an effective technique. I established through trial and error that I didn't need to laugh for long. I found that if I laughed for 5 minutes I could then enjoy a calm rest of the night. Happily I also established that the laugh can be very quiet so that my own problem-solving did not become problem-creating for my neighbors.

In this refinement, as you develop your morning laughing practice you can laugh any laugh until it becomes the real thing. You can play with your different laughing vowels or just laugh. My midnight laughing had demonstrated that very clearly. What's more, you will find when you persevere with this practice that the amount of time it takes to be able to access your genuine, good-natured laugh becomes shorter and shorter. If you keep your practice going you find you can access your own spontaneous, genuine laugh in a nano-second, i.e. immediately. In your Laughing Buddha practice, the important factor is to do your practice regularly and consistently. You need to do this to wake up your own Laughing Buddha within.

Although jokes have played no part in any of these practices, external sources of good-natured mirth can be invaluable. YouTube is an excellent resource: the Russian newsreader and the 13 bears, or the German weather reporter and her unexpected glimpse of a colleague are both perfect examples. Once they've started laughing, everything then acts as a trigger, their imaginations get unlocked and their laughter reflex becomes almost uncontrollable. "This I believe to be the chemical function of humor: to change the character of our thought", said Dr. Lin Yutang.

What both YouTube examples show and Dr. Yutang observed is that the laughing makes everything else funnier.

Everyone on the self-development path is accustomed to doing actions to promote their health, wellbeing and happiness, so there is a clear logic to laugh first in order to be able to find the funny. Everyone who has done a breath-based meditation in yoga, in relaxation or in ante-natal classes has already had the experience of doing an activity in order to produce a required result. The principle behind the Laughing Buddha laugh is exactly the same and is about choosing to develop our good-natured and joyful self without external props. The more you practice, the more your own Laughing Buddha wakes up.

Hopefully you can do it now as you read this. The progression is to start with your smile and then play with your laugh. Can you do it now? Relax, breath, smile, and let your breath out with a good-natured chuckle.

'The smiling practice technique you teach has transformed my life and I rarely walk around with a growly face these days. I am eternally thankful to you for this.'

You are now ready for the Barefoot Doctor's second exercise.

Exercise Sequence 2

Conjure the smile of the Laughing Buddha precisely as in exercise 1, breathing slowly, body relaxed all the while, and press firmly on the tendon on the soft side of the wrist leading into the bone at the base of the palm on the little finger side of the hand, at the wrist bracelet, directing the pressure towards the little finger. Maintain the press for three slow breaths, release and repeat on the other hand. This is the 'spirit door' point on the heart energy line or meridian, stimulation of which is similar in effect to taking 2.5 mg of Valium, in that it mildly sedates the raging mind and induces a state of peacefulness, openheartedness and willingness to laugh.

Next, visualize the smile rooted between your legs and extending way beyond the tops of your ears, turn into first a chuckle, then a full-blown laugh, until internally, it feels as if your whole body is laughter in motion.

Again, ever so lightly contemplate the Laughing Buddha to whom this laugh belongs, until you momentarily become the laugh of the Laughing Buddha.

Chapter 3. I don't feel like laughing.

'It's time to take laughter seriously'. Dr. Madan Kataria

Being able to laugh when you don't feel like it is essential for waking up your Laughing Buddha within. It's a crucial skill because it's at the heart of walking your talk, or more appropriately, laughing your laugh.

It is an illustration of Alistair Cooke's definition of a professional, someone who gets up and does what they've got to irrespective of how they're feeling. It is the same principle that sees us getting up in the morning and feeding the kids and doing the school run even when we are ill, hung-over or don't feel like it. When done with good heart, it is a sign of beauty and maturity. We tend to be more skilled at this than we realize and all you need do is to transfer this learning to your waking up your Laughing Buddha within.

People sometimes struggle to find their laugh because they say they're not in the mood. They often comment that it feels inauthentic, and sometimes they want to argue their case vehemently. Their point is that it is more authentic to feel what they're feeling and simply to let life unfold, rather than force themselves to try to feel better. Even a genuine, good-natured Laughing Buddha smile seems too much.

First of all, no one is forcing you to do anything. There is great truth in the martial arts approach of 'expect nothing', and deal with life as it happens. If you happen to be feeling sad, angry, hurt or depressed for instance, just feel it until the feeling passes which sooner or later it will. Even if it doesn't fully pass, that particular intensity will.

The American psychiatrist Tomas Szasz commented that the self is not something you find, it is something you create. If you are on the self-development path, you are looking to develop your 'self' in particular ways, in this case your joyful self, waking up your Laughing Buddha within.

One of the basic insights for everyone on this path is the need for awareness, or the witness. The French poet Rimbaud used the expression 'Je me vois me voir', which means 'I see myself seeing myself'. We are our own witness whenever we remember to have that awareness.

All great spiritual leaders have observed this. Eckhart Tolle's magnificent insight on page one of the 'Power of Now' comes when he realizes that, having decided he couldn't live with himself any longer, there were two aspects present, 'he' and 'himself'. That insight created space and awareness and all his revelations followed.

The importance of the witness, of being aware of how and what we're feeling as well feeling the feelings themselves, is that it introduces the possibility of choice. This approach is central to every self-development path and every spiritual quest. The simple act of witnessing provides the space for us to inquire of ourselves whether there is anything we can do to improve our current experience. Awareness allows us to be conscious rather than unconscious about what we're experiencing. It allows us to ask ourselves questions like is this necessary? Is this contrived or authentic? Is this loving? Am I happy with the way things are? Can I do something to improve the situation?

Having asked these questions, an action step is likely to present itself, and we can act on it if we so choose. The model I love and use is Awareness, Acceptance, Action. Positive, intentional choice is at the heart of self-development and to wake up your own Laughing Buddha qualities, the action steps involve smiling, laughing and kindness.

Using the mantra of relax, breathe and smile, can you smile and chuckle now?

Another reason we sometimes don't feel like laughing is because we're feeling sluggish or depressed. We might be feeling lethargic, heavy in body and spirit, and grumpy. Because there can be a strong mind-body dynamic at play, each aspect reinforces the sluggishness and heaviness in the other. This can lead to unanticipated consequences. Actors, for example, often use physical expression of emotions to create different emotions they need in a role. Dr. Kataria has discussed this with many Bollywood stars and they say that this technique is so powerful that the emotions generated in their film role can often be hard to stop. Sometimes when they have been performing tragic roles the sadness carries over into the rest of their life and can be hard to shake off.

In the 19th century American psychologist William James noticed that a person's state of mind, whether positive or negative, led to a corresponding physical expression or body behavior, and that each emotion has a corresponding physical expression. He also realized that the physical expression of any emotion creates the corresponding emotion in the mind, as the Bollywood cases confirm.

The key to breaking the cycle of sluggishness and heaviness of spirit or depression is willingness. It is willingness that motivates us to take action. Once we adopt a proactive attitude, the question becomes what action to take, and as you start waking up your own Laughing Buddha within, you develop the biggest possible toolkit to dip into.

One of the easiest actions to take is to do something physical.

For me Olivia Newton John's 'Let's Get Physical' always comes to mind with the added bonus that I can't help smiling whenever I think of her video. I happen to love to dance, not learnt steps but freestyle. I started out as one of life's ugliest ducklings on the dance floor and I was always laughed at. In the privacy of my own home I used to and still do put on boogie music and dance, shake and gyrate.

At one time I also booked myself onto a Contact Improvisation course. I thought the title meant there would be occasional physical contact. Fortunately I didn't read the course content closely because if I had I would never have gone. It wasn't occasional tiny bits of contact, it was full-on with lots of it. If I could have run away I would have, but I couldn't. After an hour of excruciating shame and awkwardness my past conditioning burnt off, I relaxed and started to enjoy it. I liberated myself from my awkwardness and now boogie publicly with abandon. It's a perfect mood improver.

Can you smile and shake a leg now?

Rather than dancing publicly, a more socially acceptable and easier action is to stretch and adjust your posture – with a soft face, which means with a smile. As ever, your Laughing Buddha smile can be very small, so small it is almost invisible, but it needs to be genuine. By making it genuine, you are connecting with your good-natured, joyful and kind self, your own Laughing Buddha within. When you put your attention onto those aspects, they inevitably and naturally start to grow. Energy always follows thought.

Because of the connection between body and mind, when you adopt the posture of a more alert and happier person, you are sending alert and happier messages via your endorphins to your brain. Measurable biochemical changes occur in your mind. Dr. Lee Berk from Loma Linda University has studied these extensively. These physiological and biochemical changes assist your psychological willingness and so your mood improves and you become happier and more alert. By initiating this kind of physical change, you start to build a genuine positive cycle which replaces the cycle of sluggishness and depression. It is called a virtuous circle. You initiate it with your awareness before taking an appropriate action – even just a smile.

Whatever your bodywork practice, it is good to remember it is neither a punishment nor a race. There are no prizes for doing it at top speed because one of the purposes is to treat it as an awareness exercise. Nor is it a punishment where you are secretly beating your body up. The best approach is with inquiry, appreciation and playfulness. If you have the time and inclination, there is a Chi Kung warm-up where you gently tap and slap your body, section by section, very slowly. In this exercise you allow yourself plenty of time just to warm up your body. You can guarantee if you bring this degree of intention to a physical routine, you will have moved a long way from any earlier sluggishness. As ever, it is essential to make a start, and the most important step to take is always the next one.

On a deeper level, the route from the head to the heart is through the body.

Joseph Campbell said he didn't believe people are looking for the meaning of life as much as they are looking for the experience of being alive. The way to shift your consciousness so that life changes from being a thinking-based activity to being an experience of being alive is to connect with your body, your physical awareness. In evolutionary terms we are wired to do this otherwise as a species we would never have made it off the African savannah. Embodying our awareness also enables us to absorb more information simultaneously and be more intuitive so that on a gut level we just know things. We need to feel our gut to have a gut feeling.

Relaxing shoulders is a good starting point because one of our biggest modern postural conditions is slumping forwards. Our shoulders are where we often store tension. Backward shoulder rolls are a natural corrective, and if you're a swimmer, spend some time doing the backstroke. If you're not a swimmer but have the space they are wonderful because besides correcting your posture, they open your chest and help your breathing. The Laughing Buddha approach is to engage your playfulness with this process and explore how many unusual and yet effective ways you can move your shoulders and relax. Putting a smile on your lips helps access your innate lightness and brings extra enjoyment. Depending on where you are and who you are with, you can develop your own spontaneous routine and bring playfulness back into your stretching, as befits your Laughing Buddha.

The more you keep your awareness alert in this process, the easier and faster you can feel the changes. Regular practice means you can put your attention on your good-natured self very quickly and by involving your body in this process you help reinforce it. Your commitment to creating good feelings in your body means you have created good feelings in your mind via your endorphins and you have turned your state of mind through 180 degrees, with no external stimulus, simply through awareness, willingness and action. This approach is central to all spiritual practices, and for it to work, all we need to do is practice regularly enough and for long enough for our brain to rewire itself and turn this approach into second nature.

The Laughing Buddha progression is smile, laugh and stretch. Can you?

'I am writing to tell you what a positive and lasting effect the Laughter Workshop has had on me.

The workshop itself was fun, but also deeply serious in intent. Since then my husband's deteriorating condition has put an almost unbearable strain on me. I have been practicing the techniques I learned that day and sometimes they transform the situation and lift my spirits. I can't begin to tell you what a difference that makes.'

It's time to get physical with the Barefoot Doctor's next exercise.

Exercise Sequence 3

With an underlying intention that by doing the following you're increasing your willingness and capacity to see the joke in absolutely everything, and physical condition permitting, stand as if you're the Laughing Buddha, and with feet close together, both feet facing forwards, legs straight, knees strong but not locked, breathing slowly and freely with body relaxed all the while, gently hang forwards from the hips. If you can easily touch the tops of your feet do so, but otherwise in no way strain, merely hold onto your legs wherever it's comfortable to do so. Allow your hamstrings to stretch and lengthen progressively more with each successive exhalation for three long breaths' worth. Then bend your knees to facilitate straightening up and come up slowly head last until standing fully upright again.

Take a moment to settle upright, then strong in the buttocks, breathing slowly and freely, body relaxed all the while, clasp your hands behind your back and roll your shoulders outwards till you feel the front upper chest stretch and lengthen. Hold the stretch for three long breaths and release slowly.

Now clasp your hands in front of you and without arching your back stretch your hands (still clasped) above your head until you feel the whole abdominal and thoracic area stretching and elongating. Hold the stretch for three long breaths, release slowly and sit down.

Next picture someone pulling the crown of your head towards the ceiling by virtue of an invisible silver thread attached to the crown of your head, until you can perceive your spine elongating. Then visualize a pair of huge invisible angel wings, remnants from before the fall, one attached to each shoulder blade, extraordinarily heavy and large as they'd need to be to get you airborne, and imagine you can feel the sheer weight of them pulling your shoulder girdle downwards and outwards, and broadening you across the upper thorax.

Finally imagine a rope tied to each of your hip bones and two tug of war teams, one on each side pulling in opposing directions until you feel your pelvic girdle broaden.

With the Laughing Buddha external stretch sequence and the internal expansion sequence above, you'll notice yourself feeling far larger already - existentially speaking at least.

Now try running the exercise 1 and 2 sequence and you'll notice it's almost difficult stopping yourself laughing aloud.

Chapter 4. Laugh for a reason.

"Be optimistic. It feels better" The Dalai Lama.

There is almost always a reason to laugh. The most important reason to laugh is because it lifts our spirits and makes us feel better. Laughing is liberation. It can even be ecstatic. The fact there are many other benefits from laughing makes the case even more compelling. This peculiarly Western obsession with seriousness needs to be replaced immediately by laughing lots.

Often the first thing we need to do is to give ourselves permission to enjoy. The second is to give ourselves additional permission to express that enjoyment. When we are on holiday, at a party or being entertained it is culturally acceptable for us to relax, smile and laugh. By contrast, walking along the street in a relaxed way, smiling and chuckling to yourself is unusual to say the least. Getting together in large groups to do it in public is so unusual it is almost inconceivable. Yet in other parts of the world hundreds and thousands of people do so regularly, whether in laughter yoga clubs in India or evening open-air square dancing in cities like Zhaoqing in China. All these cultural norms are arbitrary and when we are ready to be inquiring and courageous enough to develop our own individuality, we can start to develop our own authentic life. We can choose to develop kindness and spontaneity. As a further step we can choose specifically to enjoy life as much as possible.

In mythological terms, Graf von Durkheim talked about how when you're on a journey heading to a point on the horizon and the longer you travel, the further away that point becomes, you realize that the purpose of the journey is the journey itself. Probably every ancient culture in the world has had this insight of enjoying the process and yet somehow it is often a timely reminder for each of us as we get caught up in the business of our life. Because laughing increases our enjoyment of the process, that is probably the most fundamental reason for awakening your own Laughing Buddha within. You are engaging in an activity whose outcome is supported and advocated by many cultural traditions, especially ancient ones.

When we make a change in how we live it is always because we have new evidence. The evidence might be science, history and myth, other people's stories or our own direct personal experience, but what it does is give us reasons for starting to do things differently. We always have a reason for our thoughts, feelings and behavior. We have an intention behind every action and the quality of our intention helps color our experiences. As you wake up your Laughing

Buddha within, the colors of your experiences will become vibrant.

As ever, the way you do it is by doing it.

As we realize that we don't need to wait for something funny to make us laugh and that the laughing itself makes everything funnier, this itself becomes a good reason to laugh more. In the way William James described, life becomes more enjoyable, and as our own life becomes more enjoyable, that quality ripples out to others. People around us benefit too. This benefit is not restricted to our nearest and dearest because as recent Harvard studies show, this is contagious even with strangers.

Of course, there are many other Laughing Buddha benefits if you do not feel convinced by the prospect of enjoying your life more. Science and medicine have both been active with research into laughter benefits, and the list of benefits gets longer every year. One of the earliest cases was Norman Cousins' experience which he first wrote about in his New England Journal of Medicine article (Dec 1974) and his 1979 book, both titled 'Anatomy of an Illness'. His story is becoming better and better known, and one of his key discoveries when he was suffering debilitating pain from his ankolysing spondalitis, a potentially severe deterioration of the spine, was that 10 minutes of genuine belly laughter could produce at least 2 hours of pain-free sleep. His book is eloquent, short, and still available today.

How many more reasons do we need?

Fortunately there are many more. Additional reasons are validated by the latest neuro-science. The knack is to make a point of enjoying the 'small' things in life. The importance of these 'small' things is that what's important is valuing and enjoying them. Often in retrospect a 'small' thing that goes well is actually a 'big' thing because of the enjoyment you experience. By spending more time appreciating and enjoying what appear to be small things, modern neuro-science and neuro-plasticity show that we are rewiring our brains and developing new ways of interacting with the world. Again, we have this confluence of ancient wisdom and modern science to help give us good reason to wake up our Laughing Buddha. All the smiling and laughing practices predispose us to enjoy and appreciate more.

Now is a good moment for you to practice your mantras, to relax, breathe, smile and chuckle!

The latest research also includes the 2011 Oxford University study into the benefits of laughing. Besides being known to help conditions such as heart disease, eczema, rheumatoid arthritis, allergy, diabetes type 2, bronchitis and weight loss, it also shows that laughing helps with the rising Western epidemic of depression. I first came across this connection in 2002 when listening to the radio on my way to the University of the West of England. I heard a news piece about Dr. Koutek, an Austrian psychiatrist who had started using the sound of spontaneous laughter in his treatment of patients with depression. Further research into laughter's natural contagiousness led me to the trail of neuro-scientist Professor Sophie Scott at University College London. The sound of genuine laughter is a natural anti-depressant, and listening to it as well as practicing it helps to keep your mood buoyant and resilient. Listening to it also helps develop your own Laughing Buddha practice as your psyche is responding positively to the sound of laughing.

The theme of depression and using laughing as an uplifting counter-measure is part of Belachew Girma's story. He featured in a BBC Radio 4 news piece in 2003 when he knelt on his prayer mat in a corner of Meskel Square in Addis Ababa and laughed for two hours. His view was that in his country and elsewhere, life was full of stress. He himself had suffered catastrophic personal and financial loss, and in a time and place of social and political uncertainty he said

"Please let us communicate by smiling". He used the slogan, 'laughter, love, peace for all human beings'.

I was struck by the idea of laughing non-stop for two hours and although I already had developed my own nascent laughing yogi practices, I wondered what it was like to laugh that long. I had already practiced my morning, midnight and evening laughing but the prospect of two hours intrigued me and I resolved to explore this. It became the backbone of my 'sustained chuckle' laughing yogi technique.

In the Osho tradition there is the 'Mystic Rose' meditation, a three-week process involving three hours practice per day, and the first week is laughter. This is a group activity so you have the sound of other people's laughing and its natural infectiousness to help you laugh that long. What intrigued me was the possibility of laughing for a long time without any external influences at all, laughing for the sake of laughing. I used my car to practice in and on one journey I kept a laugh going non-stop, one breath after the next, for an hour. When I arrived at the university campus to give a lecture on the benefits of laughter, I felt that I could definitely speak from experience and it was exhilarating.

The next step was to go into a recording studio, an even more difficult environment than driving as there are even fewer external influences. There are no other quirky drivers to be stimulated by, just stony-faced technicians. I found the technique is simply to chuckle in a good-natured way on each out-breath. Volume comes and goes, as do moments of genuine hilarity when images flash to mind which fuel an eruption of mirth. But in the in-between moments when nothing particularly funny was in my mind, I just kept chuckling. The key was willingness to keep going, one chuckle at a time, like a meditative activity. A CD of two twenty minute tracks of solo unassisted laughter was the result which people now use to practice with.

This is another perfect moment for you to practice?

It is empowering to be able to laugh and access your own intrinsic joyful nature at any second you choose, for as long as you like, in any circumstances. Whether your reasons are physical, emotional, psychological, social or spiritual, your Laughing Buddha practice will benefit every aspect of life. There is always a reason to laugh.

The progressive Laughing Buddha trail is to smile, practice your laugh, stretch and chuckle on the out-breath.

'What a total relief to get out of my head and just let go.

Really really letting go with the laughing...my cheeks and tummy were aching after so much!!!

Thank you. Amazing, after the workshop I seemed to have real energy coming from within and a sense of calm. So, I will practice this amazing gift.'

You are now ready for the Barefoot Doctor's next exercise.

Exercise Sequence 4

Sit comfortably, relax your body, breathe slowly and freely, gently grab hold of your lower front ribs on each side by carefully working your fingertips up and under till you've traction, and prize the ribcage apart a few millimeters at first, then a few centimeters. Keep breathing throughout. After three slow breaths release on an exhalation and spend a few moments enjoying the sensation of relief, comfort and warmth radiating from your diaphragm.

Next run exercise sequence 1 to 3, visualizing the inner smile, the inner laugh, the Laughing Buddha stretch sequence and the internal expansion.

Finally, with each exhalation, make the sound, 'HA-HA-HA-HA-HAAAAH', landing strongly on the opening 'H' each time.

Chapter 5. Laughing as liberation.

'You have to let go of the life you thought you were going to lead, and let life live through you.' Joe Hoare

Laughing is a here and now activity and therefore is a path to ecstasy. When we laugh deeply, we become fully immersed in the present moment. Our laughing fills our whole consciousness and we're unable to read, analyze, read maps, talk, and sometimes we even fall down. I've seen someone perform an elegant and controlled descent, falling gracefully to the ground in a session when they've been laughing, as the Bushmen of the Kalahari are known to do.

This is also known as letting go and as you wake up your Laughing Buddha within you learn to do this in a nano-second. The psychological place you enter is one which in western culture we often miss. It is the in-between place, that gap in our thinking consciousness which is in-between thoughts and in-between feelings. With practice, people who meditate get to know this place well because it is the place of stillness, the foundation of our ability to be the master and not the slave of our head. It is where we become the witness and cultivate our ability to be aware of ourselves as well as be ourselves. With practice you'll come to realize it is not a tiny place but an enormous one.

It is not a place I remember being taught or even introduced to in my formal education, I had to find it for myself as I suspect most of us have to do. When we visit this place regularly, it helps us take command of our life and become the captain of our soul.

In your practice this space opens up with every genuine laugh. As you consciously wake up your Laughing Buddha within you can visit it whenever you choose. Your laughing also influences the character of the space and you become its initiator and creator, not just the witness. You color it vividly with your own palate of delight and joy, and the space becomes vibrant and sometimes ecstatic. Ecstasy is liberation, and it can be silent.

Can you do a Laughing Buddha laugh now?

My first ecstatic laughing liberation came when I was on a voice retreat with Chris James at Bedales many years ago. I had experienced spontaneous laughter many times before. For years with one particular partner we were regularly visited by the laughing spirits just before sleep and we'd lie in bed laughing uncontrollably for minutes at a stretch. It was a surprise and a delight every time and even now brings back warm and tender memories.

On the retreat it was a different but similarly unexpected visitation. When you free your voice you liberate your soul and in that process, magic happens. Part of the retreat included several meditations a day and so we were in a large circle with our eyes closed, deep in our own process.

Suddenly I realized I wanted to laugh. I was appalled at the prospect of disturbing everyone else's meditation, and I was horrified because I was still in the mindset that meditation had to be silent and serious to be effective.

All I knew was that my urge to laugh was getting stronger and undeniable. Even though this urge to laugh was becoming irresistible I had enough presence of mind to ride the wave and not be taken over by it. However I knew I needed to laugh irrespective of the consequences. I took a specific decision not to resist this experience and to allow it to happen. I started to laugh helplessly, and to my surprise and relief, silently. I just laughed and laughed, rocking backwards and forwards without a squeak emerging from my lips, or anyone else's meditation being disturbed.

I was having a kundalini-rising experience, without knowing that's what it was.

It lasted a long time and gradually subsided and by the time the meditation was over I was back from this journey and no one had seen or heard a thing. I had experienced many things simultaneously in that meditation, including the power of the silent laugh and that special place that exists in-between letting go and being out-of-control. The key Laughing Buddha insight is that you can let go and still be present, and it is a place of bliss. Usually when we laugh helplessly we cut ourselves off because it is such a strong inner experience but for those who can develop it, there is a subtle place where you can still be aware as well as letting go.

In spirit this is the Taoist wobbly man exercise.

Another process comes into play as your practice starts to wake up your Laughing Buddha within. As you start to be able to laugh genuinely on demand and become more aware and appreciative, you start to develop the ability to create these in-between spaces whenever you choose. As always, the more you practice, the easier it becomes until you find you can move into a genuinely joyful open-hearted state whenever you choose. This state affects both your thoughts and your feelings and you find you can move from kind thought to warm feeling and warm feeling to kind thought with increasing ease, very quickly, whenever you choose. I have even been able to move between competitor to healer on the squash court within a second or two. As every sage, master and student of psychology knows, being in control of your psychological state and being able to choose how to respond to any given set of circumstances, however dreadful, is a place of complete and final liberation. This is what Victor

Frankl experienced in the death camps and described in his book 'Man's search for meaning'. This is what you can do as you wake up your Laughing Buddha within, and you can learn these skills not through deprivation and hardship, but in a positive psychology way by focusing on and increasing your joyfulness.

The process of joyfulness gets better the more you practice. Can you relax, breath, smile and chuckle now?

To help in your own liberation process, dance and movement can play a big role. Teachers can arrive in surprising guises and one of mine is a friend who long before I knew him broke his back and is now in a wheelchair. He was told he'd never be able to do things like lift a glass to his lips and instead of accepting that, he took it as a challenge. He now has much greater physical abilities than anyone ever considered possible and is a respected teacher of zen and satipatthana. The basis of all his improvements came from exploring the quality of physical looseness. We all hold tension in our bodies and where and how we do this affects our consciousness and behavior. As you change your body, you change your mind, your whole mind.

My own further exploration led me to realize the further importance of freeing tension in the neck, head and face. It is very hard to let go of your thinking process if you can't let go of your thinking apparatus. Conversely, a very good way to let go of your head and relax your thinking process is to explore gentle and spontaneous head, neck and face movements. As ever, these are best practiced with a soft face and gentle smile to melt away any tension. Think of them as facial gymnastics. They are a light and playful addition to your Laughing Buddha resource kit.

If you find you struggle to smile, do the pencil in the teeth exercise we mentioned earlier and look at yourself in the mirror. Provided you do this with willingness and a fake-it-till-you-make-it attitude, the sight of ourselves looking slightly ridiculous prompts genuine mirth and makes it easier for us to experience an even greater liberation, laughing at ourselves.

Genuine laughter is naturally joyful and joyfulness connects us strongly to the magic of the present moment. On a spiritual level, on top of all the physical and bio-chemical benefits, when you laugh in a genuine and good-natured way, you are engaging in a heart-opening and connecting activity. Being open-hearted and connected is liberating for yourself and others. As you connect with your own good nature you can more easily connect with others in this same way and, as Marianne Williamson observed, when we liberate ourselves, we give others permission to do the same.

People's faces change when they do this. Even the most deeply-lined and anxious-looking face transforms when they laugh in this genuine and good-natured way. By making a specific connection with their own genuine good-nature they experience a freedom from their story with past fears and future worries, and an exquisite gentleness appears. It often appears gradually, a new fresh person being liberated, a heavy weight being put down and the carrier standing a little uncertainly as they experience a moment or eight of psychological and spiritual freedom. It is a tenderizing moment for everyone because you're in the presence of a possible transformation of someone's psyche. You're witnessing and helping them to experience a way of being they're unused to and have possibly never experienced before. They are experiencing liberation. Sometimes when people experience this they embrace the implications in an instant. With that simple Laughing Buddha practice, they have liberated and transformed their consciousness, and this immediately affects the rest of their life.

'Thank you Joe - not sure I could have gotten through this year without such inspiration.......to laugh again at all the right and 'wrong' moments.' (Grace)

The practice is building on your initial smile, stretch and chuckle framework to include letting your head go, and starting to explore your inner realm. Can you laugh silently? Can you laugh and still be present?

The Barefoot Doctor's next exercise extends your own liberation.

Exercise Sequence 5

No matter what you're liberating yourself from, at the root, you're freeing yourself of the internal drama you've concocted about the game of life and your perceived position in it. This drama is acted out by way of a dialogue occurring incessantly in the prefrontal lobes of the brain, a dialogue involving all your various sub-personalities, each of them describing various opinions and views, together comprising an ever-shifting, invariably dubious perspective based almost entirely on a set of spurious, subjective criteria, but which you nonetheless tend to delude yourself into confusing with reality itself.

And there's no way to stop it. It appears to be an essential function of this front part of the brain: to create fiction so convincing you confuse it for what's actually going on.

However by following the following carefully, you'll afford yourself an optional mode in which internal silence, stillness and absence of drama reigns, that if chosen with regularity will, by and by, attenuate the noise in the forebrain enough to free you of your delusions fairly permanently, and if you combine this with the preceding exercise sequences on a regular basis, as will be presently suggested, you'll soon find yourself able to laugh yourself free of the drama in a jiffy.

Press sensitively but firmly into the center of your forehead just above the eyebrow line as if your fingertip has magical bone-penetration powers until you feel as if you're penetrating all the way to the midbrain region. Then do the same with the point that lies directly under the base of the skull in the depression between the spine and the skull caused by tipping our head back.

Next close your eyes (after reading this) and visualize the inside of your skull as the interior of a secret cave high up in the sacred mountain peaks. Subtly tilt your head back a tad and let your whole mind slide rearwards along the floor of the cave, until it's nestling up against the rear interior wall of the cave (skull), and picture it sitting there in the form of the Laughing Buddha, laughing (funnily enough, pardon the pun) as she or he gazes off into infinity through the mouth of the cave (situated roughly at the previously pressed point on the forehead), watching unconcerned as thoughts drift past the cave mouth like clouds passing from one side of the night sky to the other, devoid of any urge to jump on one and find out where it leads.

Once you've grown familiar with this procedure, run sequences 1 to 4 precisely and with practice you'll find yourself liberated by laughter at every turn.

Chapter 6. Laughing from the inside out.

'Joy is inside you. Not in the attainment of things desired, nor in the achievement of goals made, but in the simple feeling that lies within you. Know that this joy is unaffected by outer circumstance, and joy will be yours forever.' Unknown Zen.

As you awaken your Laughing Buddha within, you start laughing from the inside out. This means your laugh becomes an expression of good-natured enjoyment and joyfulness rather than a response to external stimulus. Even if you're not feeling particularly good-natured or joyful, you can laugh to boost these qualities. The first time Dr. Kataria, the founder of Laughter Yoga, and I met in Birmingham in 2002, we swapped notes. I mentioned to him that I used the phrase 'fake it till you make it' to get people laughing, and he said he did too. This is now one of the key lines in laughter yoga and Laughing Buddha practices and means that your ability to laugh is an internally generated activity. It comes from within you and not from an external prompt of something being funny. You laugh to activate your laughing self and be able to laugh more.

With practice, you can also learn to laugh in the face of adversity. The recent short documentary 'The Best

Medicine' about Jon, who has a brain tumor and used to be prone to fits of rage, shows this. Through his involvement in the Bristol laughter sessions, he taught himself to laugh at the things in his life that aren't funny. He started with the smiling exercises and kept progressing from there.

Of course, as we have already discussed, external stimuli like jokes, humor and life's quirkiness can all elicit anything from a chuckle to a big belly laugh, and it is lovely and healthy that they do. It is important to use these resources and respond to them as much and as often as we can. It is helpful to spend time deliberately being surrounded by good news, by appreciation, by positive stories and images. This is especially true when done instead of absorbing the usual daily barrage of global and domestic bad news. In his self-cure, for example, Norman Cousins specifically watched videos to make him laugh. At the very least, watching or listening to a comedy lightens our mood and entertains and distracts us and as we have already seen, the more we laugh, the more likely we are to laugh more.

Sometimes people who spend time in life and death situations use dark humor as a safety valve. There are apocryphal stories of doctors working in disaster zones who make what might seem to outsiders as inappropriate and callous jokes about the predicament of the people they're caring for. The underlying reality is that it is a coping mechanism. I experienced an example of this in a group of carers I was working with. For those not familiar with a carer's role, their responsibilities can be overwhelming as they might be the main carer for 24 hours a day. They need to be ingenious and flexible to enjoy their moments of relief. In one group a carer said that in their family they use the news as a source of relief, and whatever the headline, they cheer. Although this might sound callous to those of us who aren't walking in those particular shoes, the clever thing they'd done was consciously to structure laughter into their daily practice. All the other carers in that group commended him because they all knew about relentless pressure and the importance of safety valves.

On the science trail, the avid researcher Dr. Lee Berk's work shows some surprising effects from this kind of activity when he measured raised endorphin levels after prolonged mirthful laughter 12-24 hours later. When you are in Laughing Buddha mode, this gives your awareness a definite bio-chemical trail. If your system has raised endorphin levels, it is feeling better than if it does not. For example, it might even mean you wake up in the morning in a good mood. How aware of this are you? What connection and communication do you have between your body and your mind? If you are full of improved health, how aware are you of this and how much do you allow this to influence your mood and attitude?

Because our brain likes patterns and routine, it can be unfortunately easy to allow gloomy or depressive thoughts to have a stronger and longer-lasting effect than they deserve. If the majority of our information intake ranges from the dispiriting to the horrific, it is easy to live in an unconscious and habitual state of anything from mild uneasiness to anxiety, depression or fear. In this scenario we might stay a bit low-spirited until some happy external event occurs which perks us up.

As you develop your Laughing Buddha practices you realize you can lift your spirits at any time. The more you practice, the more you put yourself in control of your consciousness. In the early phases of all self-expression practices it is essential to do them physically.

Now is a good moment to practice?

To allow the changes to percolate in and become part of your being, you have to practice your good-natured smiling and laughing with the same regularity you hopefully use for your yoga or meditation. As your practices start to develop deep roots you find you can wake up your Laughing Buddha within merely with your awareness.

Two further refinements help this.

When I was running the Shaftesbury Overtone Chanting group we spent years exploring many dimensions of toning (sustained use of vowel sounds) and acapella improvisation. The journey started with freeing the natural voice and after a year or so we started to explore silent sound. We explored it first as if we were physically making the sounds with our mouths fully open and our bodies alive and expressive, and we interspersed this with usual vocalizing. Gradually we began to explore silent sound where we didn't move our mouths or bodies at all and concentrated our attention on our inner ear and our imagination. At this time we were also exploring healing sound circles or sound baths where one person would go into the middle of the circle and be 'bathed' by the sounds from the group. The feedback we started getting was that people in the middle had a more profound experience from the silent sound and the most profound experience when there was no apparent sound or movement at all. In this way everything was happening at an intentional and vibrational level. What we had done through our years of practice was to produce an effect through our intention.

The carry-over to your Laughing Buddha practice is that after a time you can internalize your mirth, and feel and generate an effect in exactly this way.

I now have a somatic sensation of my own inner Laughing Buddha. I hear the laugh in my inner ear and experience it in my body. I feel it in my hara, just below my navel in that place identified by martial arts as the center of our personal power. I also experience a softening around my heart but that is secondary to my hara sensation.

I became aware of this sensation some time after doing my regular morning Laughing Buddha practices, which by then had extended into daytime and evening practices. I came to realize how grounding these practices are because not only were my spirits being lifted and my mood improved, I was also experiencing more control over my quality of life. All I need do now is put my awareness on my laughing hara and I experience an immediate lift in spirit and mood and can access and express my Laughing Buddha laugh at any time. With additional practice of laughing on the inside I find I experience the same degree of lightening of mood and spirit as if I'd laughed out loud.

I use this practice every day when I'm out and about. I smile invisibly at random passers-by. On one occasion I was on the train in Spain, on holiday. I had the usual clutter of bags and there was no space to stack them. There was a hatchet-faced woman sitting opposite me so in a gentle way I gave her an invisible smile because it looked as if she needed it. A few seconds later, I almost fell off my seat in surprise when she smiled and offered to make space for my bags. That was not the reason I'd given her an invisible smile and yet it had the effect of eliciting spontaneous kindness. To me, that was synchronicitous proof of the power of kindness. We both experienced a moment of quiet joy.

With practice you can attune your awareness to moments of improved physical wellbeing, let alone joy. You can then use this awareness to lighten your thoughts and allow them to be colored by your choice rather than by circumstances or habit. This internal liberation is a step to greater wellbeing and enjoyment.

Through Fredrickson's recent and extensive positive psychology studies we also know that besides increasing our pain threshold and lifting our spirits, two other benefits of stimulating positive emotion are to improve our ability to think clearly, and to think clearly for longer. As you wake up your Laughing Buddha within it means you are tuning your antennae into good and encouraging news, and this helps keep your good-natured reservoir topped up. You will also think better. In short, you enjoy more and perform better.

Besides awareness, the other quality that helps build this inner reservoir is appreciation. One of the changes it is often hardest to make is to replace focusing on the negative with focusing on the positive. There is a genuine psychological hard-wiring that your Laughing Buddha practices have to overcome. The qualities of appreciation and celebration lift your mood and bring a smile to your lips. Conversely as you'll know from your practices, putting the smile on your lips will lift your mood and lighten your spirit. Doing this repeatedly builds the virtuous circle of celebration, expression, improved wellbeing and awareness which can repeat endlessly.

In this way your mood and your quality of life becomes centered round your own awareness which you can lighten at any time with your Laughing Buddha smile.

'A wonderful journey into releasing my bottled up emotions. Took me back to my natural self.'

As your practice builds, can you feel any changes in your body, in your open-heartedness and in a lightness of spirit?

Can you also start consciously to radiate this subtle internal joyfulness to people you meet in your day-to-day life?

Exercise Sequence 6

With an underlying intention that by following the following you'll be reinforcing the notion that it's OK for you to be laughing constantly, whether internally or externally, no matter what, sit comfortably, body relaxed, breathing slowly and freely and press lightly but with intent on the crown of your head, directly above the tops of your ears, again imagining your fingertips to have the mysterious power to penetrate bone, until you can feel the effect in the midbrain region. Hold for three slow breaths and return your hand to your lap. Now visualize a golfball size sphere of brilliant white light spinning at the speed of light in a clockwise direction a thumb's width distance above the crown for the length of three slow breaths, and you'll activate what the ancient Taoists called, 'the spirit of positive vitality'.

Now press in the dead center of the breastbone, again as if penetrating the bone, till you feel the sensation all the way back on the frontal aspect of your thoracic spine, by which time you'll be feeling your whole chest relax and soften.

Next run sequences 1 to 5 and practice all daily, and you'll see how much lighter of spirit and lighter of heart you're starting to feel as you and the Laughing Buddha archetype merge identities progressively more.

Chapter 7. Keep on turning up.

"Follow your bliss and the universe will open doors where there were only walls.' Joseph Campbell

As you wake up your Laughing Buddha within, miracles happen.

Grumpiness becomes a thing of your past. For those of us with ingrained grumpy streaks, and worse, this benefit alone is worth the Laughing Buddha practice. You might still have dark moods and low spirits, sleepless moments and troubles, but you don't linger there. Churchill said 'If you're going through hell, keep going' and although the image of Churchill the bulldog as a Laughing Buddha might be too surreal to entertain, his insight is helpful. By continually coming into the present with your Laughing Buddha smile you allow yourself space and separation from your story. You improve your mood and lift your spirit.

Here in the west we live in such a state of distraction that being present is an altered state of consciousness. Being present and fully engaged in the here and now often feels unnatural because we live in an era of 24 hour media and social media frenzy which we are constantly encouraged to engage with. Although this can be exciting and modern, it can also be distracting because our attention is always being pulled by the loudest noises. It becomes difficult to hear the sound over the din, and to experience that 'still small voice of calm'. In this unsettled state, until we learn to master our thinking process and what we put our attention on, we also tend to either pore over the past or worry about the future and so create an endless wheel of regret and anxiety.

Laughing Buddha practices cut through this cycle instantly because once you decide to take charge of your consciousness, they expand the present moment in a joyful way. This is 'turning up'.

One way to turn up is to adapt the classic watching the breath meditation into the one-breath meditation. Because so many Laughing Buddha practices involve vocalizing, like laughing for instance, they are all carried on our breath. Breathing practices fit into Laughing Buddha practices easily and naturally in the same way they fit into laughter yoga and every other practice. For instance the common ground between laughter yoga and yoga is breathwork. Awareness of our breath as an anchor is probably the oldest and most effective meditative technique, and the easiest way to access this technique is to chunk it up into tiny pieces. The smallest unit, the smallest piece is always 1.

An illustration of this model can be seen from about as different a context as is possible to imagine and comes from Joe Simpson in his book 'Touching the Void.' For those unfamiliar with his story, he was with his climbing partner in South America and his partner had to cut his rope. Joe fell a hundred feet or so, broke his legs but survived. His ordeal then began because he realized that to stay alive he had to get back to camp, and that meant crawling a very long distance. He managed it over the next few days with minutes to spare before the others broke camp to leave. He did so by chunking up his progress into small pieces of agonizing crawling followed by rewarding himself with a rest. In order to keeping going, he realized the key was chunking it up.

This model applies to breath meditation. To make it as easy as possible, chunk it up into a one-breath meditation which means keeping your attention on your breath for one complete breath. One complete breath is the pause before the in-breath, the in-breath itself, the pause before the out-breath, and the slightly longer out-breath. The almost invariable effect of this technique is to cut through the chattering monkey-mind, slow down your stream of consciousness, give a tiny glimmer of space and expand your awareness of here and now.

A perfect one-breath meditation is to smile, take a big breath, exhale slowly and feel the exquisite quality of your out-breath. Sense it as intensely as you can. The more you practice, the more you feel. Can you do one now?

The Laughing Buddha twist on this meditation came originally from my Chi Kung practice and the exercise, taken from The Way of Energy, called 'standing like a tree'. Standing exercises might sound easy, pointless and boring but you won't think that once you've explored them. They are vigorous and demanding, and the added tip from Master Lam Kam Chuen was to smile during these exercises. Adding the smile brings the dimension of enjoyment to self-development activities which we sometimes take so seriously they stop being enjoyable. Except for masochists and their special relationship with pain, when activities stop being enjoyable they become harder to persevere with. This is de-motivating and contributes to us giving them up. When you wake up your Laughing Buddha within you look to enjoy every process. You look to bring sparkle and enjoyment to everything you do. You look to expand your open-heartedness. Adding a smile to your one-breath meditation helps in every way.

As you do your soft-face smile, notice what difference it makes to your attention. There is inherent joyfulness in being alive which your smile amplifies and this acts as a reward for you 'turning up'. Smiling in this way increases delight in the present moment and possibly adds a grounded exuberance which gives the present moment even more piquancy. This gives an in-built incentive to repeat the practice and keep turning up. You realize you can follow one one-breath meditation with another, for as many breaths as you choose.

Can you do a Laughing Buddha smiling one-breath meditation now? Can you do it with a big smile on your face and in your heart? Can you feel a difference by doing that?

The next step is to practice your Laughing Buddha laugh as a way of turning up. You can think of it as either your sustained chuckle or laugh-at-will, and it develops from your one-breath meditation. Instead of just breathing out silently, you start breathing out with an open-mouthed sigh. This might cause you to yawn, which is excellent because it relaxes you even further. The more you relax your breathing so it is coming from your belly and you're breathing abdominally, the greater the relaxation.

Abdominal breathing is an excellent skill to re-learn. When I went to my first ever Mind Body Spirit festival I had a Kirlian photograph taken, which incidentally I still possess. At the end of the interpretation the therapist said: 'and learn how to breathe'. Of course at the time this meant the princely sum of zero but I never forgot her comment, and years later as I started to come to my senses I learnt to breathe abdominally again. This has been a boon with unexpected benefits. Besides being a superb stress-buster, it is also a pleasure enhancer. It opens the doors to hours of tantra, an unexpected benefit to Laughing Buddha practices.

I am indebted to Peter Aziz for insights in his little gem of a book 'Shamanic Healing'. In it he talks about and recommends the one-minute breath, 30 seconds in and 30 seconds out. This takes a lot of practice, it took me about 3 months of regular night-time practice, but with patience it is feasible and underpins other practices including your Laughing Buddha laugh. You use your Laughing Buddha morning laugh to bring your attention into the present moment. Combine it with your one-breath meditation.

As we discussed earlier, if you are experiential you can just laugh. If you are more visual, use your imagination and memory to bring happy images to your mind's eye to trigger your laugh. When you add it to your one-breath meditation you are strengthening the process because you are expanding your lung capacity at the same time. Laughing Buddhas have big breaths.

Can you do a Laughing Buddha one-breath laugh? It's fine to start by doing a one-breath meditation, but can you then add a chuckle to your exhalation?

The science that underlies this re-programming is neuro-plasticity. Contrary to the prevailing urban legend in my youth, our brain never stops growing. When we engage regularly in a new and creative process from figuring something out to composing a symphony, our brain grows new neural pathways in response. The first time we do something new, like learning to relax, there is a flash of communication between existing neurons. Our brain is adjusting to this novelty. Two or three times after we've repeated this, our brain starts to link up the gaps between these communicating neurons with branch-like structures called dendrites. These dendrites grow in response to our repeated stimulus and in this way our brain changes in ways that can now be measured. Hard science underpins neuro-plasticity. One reason why things become second nature to us is because through our regularity we have established a dendritic structure and neural pathways in our brain. Our brain is wired to behave and respond in a particular way.

Happily this same science applies to learning new good habits like smiling and relaxing. It used to be thought that we needed to follow a practice regularly every day for 30 days to establish a new habit. Current thinking has brought this down to 20 days as in Deepak Chopra's 20-day meditation challenge. Irrespective of the precise length of time it takes, all we need do is introduce little changes and use them regularly for our brains and consequently our outlook and behavior to start to change.

In this way each visit to your Laughing Buddha heartland is like bringing another pebble to your cairn. It might only be a tiny pebble but with each visit you replenish stocks that are otherwise being gradually eroded. Each visit makes your cairn bigger and more visible to your awareness. You make it more robust and better able to endure life's storms and with a bit of canny building it provides you with shelter in which to see them out. You need frequent visits initially because you have to mark out the space and set the foundations. The first few visits make little impression because the stones are so small they are almost invisible but after a while you start to realize your cairn is becoming noticeable. You start to see it from a little way off and recognize it with a happy familiarity. Each visit becomes increasingly pleasurable as your cairn gets bigger. To do all this you only need to keep turning up and noticing the difference.

'Just wanted to share with you that when I got home, talking to a friend on a phone many hours later, I noticed my cheeks were rosy and sore from so much smiling. The same feeling has been present all day today.......my thoughts of the event itself was 'yes. Great fun. Really good.'...having this

silly smile on my face 24 hours later, it's now 'yes. Great fun. Truly amazing.'

Can you use your Laughing Buddha skills to turn up? To be more present?

Can you bring your smile, your relaxing body, your breathing, your chuckle, and your embodied awareness into this present moment? Can you savor it?

This next exercise from the Barefoot Doctor helps you anchor your practice.

Exercise Sequence 7

To be able to show and be present at the arising of each and every moment requires a stronger identification with that inner background presence some call the spirit, some the witness-bearer: the deepest aspect of consciousness that watches without judgement, censure or approval as your life unfolds, for all we know lifetime after lifetime. Once you're able to identify fully with this inner background presence, you're able to desist from taking life's slings and arrows personally ever again, and it's this very ability to so desist that facilitates the requisite humor to awaken the Laughing Buddha within and keep her or him awake for the duration.

And the way it's done is incredibly simple and obvious, once you know how. All you have to do is sit or stand comfortably, close your eyes, relax everything, breathe slowly and tilt backwards a tad from the hips and afford yourself the sensation of tilting your person into the back of your body, so that you feel as if you're leaning up against your own shoulder blades, the front of your spine and the hip bones and sacrum.

From here, now occupying all of you, rather than just the front part as is normal on account of our fascination for the razzle-dazzle of the external world, before you pull yourself forwards within, you suddenly notice that you're *not* the drama occurring in the front of you nor the swirl of emotions it triggers in your chest, nor even the solar plexus tension caused by the friction of resisting the new. These things are all going on up front but you are now here breathing slowly, relaxed, watching it all, rather than being it all.

Learning to be in the back of you, by daily practice, you also notice that it connects you to where you've come from: your own past and the past of all your ancestors, which comprises your true wealth and support, rather than being exclusively fixated on the future. Being supported by what got you here, where you're going tends to take care of itself.

Now combine this with exercise sequences 1 to 6 and you're almost all the way there.

Chapter 8. Be a beacon.

"Do something wonderful, people might imitate it." Albert Schweitzer.

"Every time you smile at someone, it is an action of love, a gift to that person, a beautiful thing." Mother Teresa.

Holding the Laughing Buddha frequency in day-to-day life is a gift to yourself and others. It is also a never-ending practice and like the apparently apocryphal stories of oriental martial artists who knock you over with a flick of their finger, the longer you practice the more profound it becomes. The effect of your presence grows. You only have to watch someone like the Dalai Lama to experience the effect of focused practice. In spite of all his hardships, his calm and yet bubbling presence is palpable.

We are all influencing life all the time, even when sitting alone in the most remote spot on a desert island. We can get a mystical sense of this connection when we remember Indra's net, the ancient Hindu insight that we are all dreams of the dreaming god but we are all dreaming and co-creating too. A scientific reminder is Deepak Chopra's 'I am in you and you are in me', meaning we are all energetically part of the same soup. Everything we think, do and feel has an impact and so in a subtle way we are all responsible for everything. The modern Huna system of Ho'oponopono and especially the work of Dr Hew Len demonstrate how much we influence everyone and everything around us.

Your every thought and feeling emits a frequency all the time. Can you emit a conscious Laughing Buddha good-natured frequency now?

As our presence is already a beacon the question arises, what kind of beacon do you want to be? In stark terms, is your life an example or a warning? How aware are you of the impact you're having? What kind of impact is it? Is it what we want it to be, or can we do better?

'Doing better' in self-development terms is probably the hardest practice because it covers every aspect of our life, and is never-ending. There are huge pressures on us to conform and be someone else and have their values and their approval. The path to being a beacon of authentic individuality requires us to develop particular qualities, the most important of which is probably courage. The word courage comes from the French 'coeur', which means heart. Courage requires us to put our heart into something. The definitions of courage, which include bravery and boldness, highlight the ability to confront fear, pain, uncertainty and intimidation, and act in spite of these. Courage is not the absence of fear but our ability to take a risk and put our heart into a situation even though we might get hurt and experience pain again. Courage is also a full engagement with a situation because when you risk your heart you are putting yourself, your self, on the line. This is one reason why it is such an attractive and inspiring quality.

Your Laughing Buddha practices help you build courage. You find courage by being courageous. You find it by being prepared to do something because your 'knowing' self, your witness, knows you have to irrespective of the consequences. Usually the consequences are just pain or shame and like all feelings, they too pass.

My own breakthrough came when I was no longer prepared to be bullied. I did endless mental rehearsals, screwed my existing courage up, and was prepared to face my tormentor no matter what the consequences. When the next situation arose, a magic thing happened. As I was squaring up and preparing to 'fight', I realized the subtle messages I was emitting were different from previously. I was also aware they were being received. Invisibly and yet somehow visibly, I saw my tormentor back down, and from that moment on I was never bullied again.

Authentic individuality is optimistic and requires courage because unless you are deluded, you know you will experience disappointments in your life. Somewhere inside us is a Churchillian 'never give up' place and at times we need to find it. Courage helps us bounce back. We all have a place of flexible toughness underlying the courage and optimism and your Laughing Buddha practices develop it.

Can you do a Laughing Buddha chuckle now? Can you also do a silent one?

Excitingly, there is no evidence for this authenticity and courage practice. The only way to know the truth of this is to experience it.

Along my own path I had another victory. I used to have occasional but regular heebie jeebies especially over my business or the loneliness of the pioneer. My business fell a long way into debt before it started to bounce, and pioneering is a lonely place until you learn how not to be lonely. I have de-fanged both these fears by using Laughing Buddha practices.

When any dark, brooding impulses or heaviness of spirit appear, I no longer resist. I accept them and experience them and let them pass. If they show signs of wanting to take up residence as they used to, I breathe, smile, chuckle, have a little dance with them and show them the door. They are powerless to resist. Somehow, by being positive and proactive and using these practices, magic happens. Somehow this taps into the underlying 'yes' quality of life and miracles occur. I've had this experience enough times that I now know this to be true. I know that by accepting them and not resisting, heebie jeebies pass. I've learnt not to make them into a story nor catastrophize. I've learnt slowly and the hard way, but I've learnt. And if I can, so can you.

Take a moment to relax, breathe and smile. Take another moment to radiate your Laughing Buddha vibration.

When we are younger any outlook into a future of optimism and hope is based on faith not personal experience. As we get older we have the potential to sift through our experiences and appreciate how many skills we have for bounce-back-ability and flexible toughness. We can base our outlook on direct personal experience, no matter what we've gone through. Simply being alive shows we have survival skills. This appreciation is the leading edge of Laughing Buddha practices, and we make them work by frequent regularity. As Arthur Ashe said, 'Start where you are, use what you've got, do what you can'.

In 2011 I had the pleasure of meeting Claude Anshin Thomas, a Vietnam war-veteran turned Buddhist monk. He is the author of 'At Hell's Gate – a Soldier's journey from War to Peace', the story of his journey. His life imploded after his Vietnam experiences where he was responsible for hundreds of deaths. On his return to the States, he spiralled down the path of drink and drugs and living rough till he hit rock bottom and bounced. After many years he became a Buddhist monk and is the founder of the Zaltho Foundation which helps others bounce too.

One of the insights from conversations with him was how he viewed his practices. From the outside he might appear a serene and enlightened being but for him, all that keeps him from sliding back into his abyss are his practices. He doesn't do them in a style of spiritual mastery but because they are a cornerstone of practical necessity. I found it very encouraging to hear that because to stay in my own Laughing Buddha groove I am constantly aware of the need to keep my foundations strong. I need to keep grounded to keep melting the edges of my ego. It is sometimes said that to achieve mastery of your speciality you have to put in 10,000 hours. As I looked at him I was encouraged to persevere.

When we combine courage with perseverance, our boundaries expand beyond what we might previously have thought possible. When you combine your Laughing Buddha smile with your physical looseness in a spirit of playfulness, you are creating a new paradigm for yourself. When you focus on your one-breath meditation and chuckle on the out-breath, you are using neuro-plasticity to develop your joyful individuality. When you become used to centering yourself like a perfectly aligned fulcrum, and staying present at the same time, you are developing your effectiveness. Through our interconnectedness this progression takes us from personal practice to serving others.

In this instance there is reassuring scientific evidence. One way this effect spreads is through phenomena called mirror neurons. These were discovered by Professor M. Iacoboni in experiments on monkeys reaching for food. Accidentally and providentially he discovered that the same brain cells are activated when making the action as are activated when simply watching someone else make that same action. He extended his work to the power of the smile and in 2006 he stated that merely observing a smile starts a cascade of neural activity and feelings typically associated with a smile without any direct cognitive process. This means when we see a smile, our psyche automatically responds. Immediately and effortlessly we experience a milder version of what the person smiling is experiencing. This is the science of the infectiousness of your Laughing Buddha smile.

As you progress down your Laughing Buddha path, the quality of sublimation arises. In the early days of my own waking up process, a friend told me of a breathing workshop he had attended where one of the points was that when you can breathe steadily through a painful memory it no longer imprisons you. The more I reflected on that and the more experiences I had made me realize that breathing through any strong experience gives it an added dimension. Breathing as deeply and steadily as possible through painful conversations about heart-break allows the dual aspects of expressing and processing to occur. As mentioned in the previous chapter, prolonged out-breath is a relaxing, calming, stress-busting technique. Breathing deeply and steadily through intense stimulation is a key tantric practice and turns minutes into hours. When you find you can breathe steadily and deeply through stronger and stronger sensations, your process of inner liberation is developing. Your beacon, your ability to influence for the better, is becoming more effective.

Now is another good moment to relax, breathe and smile your Laughing Buddha smile.

What might have started as a one-off experience, your first genuine good-natured on-demand smile or chuckle, can become part of your daily practice. Your first Laughing Buddha smile is then a spark that lights your flame, and as with starting any fire you have to tend it carefully at first. You might have to strike your tinder time and again before your kindling catches but with the right kindling, it will light. From then on, all you need do is tend your flame.

The Roman philosopher Plutarch said 'The mind is not a vessel to be filled, it is a flame to be kindled'. Let's all kindle ours.

Laughing Buddha practices are learnable and compatible with all other self-development practices. The quality they add is lightness. It is hard to imagine any situation where it is better to have a heavy heart. There will be situations where we experience one but that heaviness does not usually improve the situation. The path of lightness is always the path home.

Your Laughing Buddha practices are empowering because they strengthen your ability to be aware and to make conscious choices. The ability to have presence of mind and an open heart in life's ups and downs develops a sense of control and calm in the eye of the storm.

They improve your physical and mental health. The bio-chemical effects of good-natured laughter not only induce mood improvements but also help pain relief and a growing list of physical and psychological ailments.

They are fun, whether done with others or on your own. They help you enjoy life more and help you help others.

Finally, as you awaken your Laughing Buddha within, you are on a journey of re-union. You are developing a yogic union of breath with body, body with mind, mind with spirit, self with others, and self with the universe. You are connecting with your heart. In a meta-physical sense you experience re-union. You're going home.

I'd like to leave you with a story of the Golden Buddha.

A farmer was commissioned by his local temple to transport its precious clay Buddha to a neighboring temple. He loaded it onto his cart and set off. On the way, it started to rain. The clay started to run, and he could see the Buddha becoming defaced. He could do nothing to protect it. It started to rain harder and the clay started to wash away. He then noticed little gleams in the statue, and the more it rained, the more it gleamed. Little specks of gold started to show through. The gleams got bigger and bigger. Underneath the clay was a brilliant golden Buddha and as the rain washed off the clay, it revealed the golden Buddha in all its magnificence. Inside us all, underneath our clay, is a radiant Buddha. So it is with the Laughing Buddha practice. As we wash away our 'clay' we reveal our brilliant Laughing Buddha within.

The final exercise is to radiate your Laughing Buddha vibration as far as you can imagine, and then a little bit further.

Build up to this with your mantra of relax, breathe and smile. Loosen your body. Deepen your breathing. Have a good-natured chuckle as you exhale. Start to do this silently. Imagine this rippling out. Imagine this rippling in. In an almost impossible way, imagine it doing both simultaneously. And please remember to smile.

*'That magical weekend still remains with me. I can't
tell you what a difference it has made to my life. All my friends
and family have noticed the difference in me, I feel lighter and
am full of laughter and a spring in my step......*

*'......a fresh start. I just knew that the weekend was
the start of a very special journey for me
personally..............(my husband) and I continue to work
hard to repair and build a new relationship with each other,
learning from our mistakes and listening to one another.'*

Exercise Sequence 8

There's an ancient Taoist axiom, that to truly gain
something you have to first give it away. In other words, by
selflessly dedicating your joyful state of being to all
humankind, not to mention all sentient life forms, both on
this planet, and who knows, even way beyond, you gain the
gift of perpetual joy. To wit, run exercise sequences 1 to 7
diligently and finally find yourself sitting comfortably, primed
to laugh for eternity.

Now examine the soft side of your forearm and
measure approximately one plum's distance up from
(proximal to) the wrist bracelet along the groove between the
two tendons that run up the middle of the (soft side of the)
forearm, and tap here with the first two finger-pads of the

other hand 36 times, then repeat on the other arm. This induces the essence of the energy of joyfulness from the depths of your heart.

Next press your right thumb firmly yet sensitively into the centre of your left palm till it aches pleasantly, for the length of three slow breaths, then repeat on the other hand. Stimulating these points increases the willingness and capacity to both give and receive.

Finally, HA-HA-HA-HA-HAAAAH-ring so that your laughter is the laughter of the Laughing Buddha, picture the Laughing Buddha hiding behind every sentient being all 7+ billion people here and all other life forms besides, as well as the Earth itself, the moon, the other planets, the sun, the asteroids, the other solar systems and planets, the Milky Way, all the other galaxies, even the black holes and all the space between - see her or him sitting there, behind everyone and everything throughout the universe laughing as you laugh, for all eternity.

Now you've got it. Merry laughing.

For more details on the Barefoot Doctor, please visit www.barefootdoctorglobal.com

For more details of my work, please visit www.joehoare.co.uk

Printed in Great Britain
by Amazon